Help Your Child To Read

Hip-Hippo-Ray

ALLAN AHLBERG and ANDRÉ AMSTUTZ

GRANADA
London Toronto Sydney New York

Help Your Child To Read

Parents can help their children to start reading. It is not difficult, nor is it necessary to be a trained teacher. In many ways home is a better place to start than school. In school your child will share the teacher's time with 25 or 30 others. At home he can have your undivided attention.

The series HELP YOUR CHILD TO READ is a set of books for parents to share with their children. The books contain stories, rhymes and games. Also, on page 3 of each book, there are practical suggestions for parents: ways in which they can help their children to start reading.

Reading Around

Sharing books with a child is not the only way of helping him to read. Opportunities for 'reading' can be found in many places. In the home (cereal packets – alphabet spaghetti – the post – magnetic letters on fridge doors – steamed up windows) and outside (street signs – petrol station ads and prices – car numbers – shops – telephone boxes – pillar boxes – hoardings – house numbers and names).

Chat with your child about what's noticed: words, letters, numbers. Gradually he will become aware of the wealth of written language and start 'reading' some of it.

With my hand on my head
what have I here?
Those are your eye-blinkers
Hippo, dear.

Eye-blinkers,
the children say.
That's what we learnt
in school today.

What have I here ?
Ear-flappers !

With my hand on my head
what have I here?
Those are your ear-flappers
Hippo, dear.

Ear-flappers,
Eye-blinkers,
the children say.
That's what we learnt
in school today.

With my hand on my head
what have I here?
Those are your chin-choppers
Hippo, dear.

Chin-choppers,
Ear-flappers,
Eye-blinkers,
the children say.
That's what we learnt
in school today.

With my hand on my tummy
what have I here?
That is your bread-basket
Hippo, dear.

Bread-
basket

Bread-basket,
Chin-choppers,
Ear-flappers,
Eye-blinkers,
the children say.
Oh, dear – those clouds
look rather grey.

With my hand on my leg
what have I here?
Those are your knee-knockers
Hippo, dear.

Knee-knockers,
Bread-basket,
Chin-choppers,
Ear-flappers,
Eye-blinkers,
the children shout.
Ha ha – look now!
The sun's come out!

With my hand on my hoof
what have I here?
Those are your globe-trotters
Hippo, dear.

Globe-trotters,
Knee-knockers,
Bread-basket,
Chin-choppers,
Ear-flappers,
Eye-blinkers,
the children say.
That's what we learnt
in school today.

With my hand on this box
what have I here?
That is your picnic-hamper
Hippo, dear.

Picnic-hamper,
Globe-trotters,
Knee-knockers,
Bread-basket,
Chin-choppers,
Ear-flappers,
Eye-blinkers,
the children say.
Are we invited . . . ?

Hip-Hip

po-Ray!
Help!

Eye
Ear
Teeth
Tummy
Knee
Feet

Eye-blinkers
Ear-flappers
Chin-choppers
Bread-basket
Knee-knockers
Globe-trotters

Published by Granada Publishing Limited in 1983
ISBN 0 246 11857 1 (cased)
0 583 30549 0 (limp)

Granada Publishing Limited
Frogmore, St Albans, Herts AL2 2NF
and
36 Golden Square, London W1R 4AH
515 Madison Avenue, New York, NY 10022, USA
117 York Street, Sydney, NSW 2000, Australia
60 International Blvd, Rexdale, Ontario, R9W 6J2, Canada
61 Beach Road, Auckland, New Zealand

Printed and bound in Spain by
Graficas Reunidas S.A., Madrid